A bird-loving man

Rodney Williams

A bird-loving man:

haiku and tanka

with illustrations by Helen Timbury

GP

Acknowledgements

Most of the work included here first appeared in these journals: *acorn*, *American Tanka*, *Atlas Poetica*, *bottle rockets*, *Chrysanthemum*, *Eucalypt*, *Famous Reporter*, *FreeXpresSion*, *Frogpond*, *The Gean Tree*, *Ginyu*, *Haiku Canada Review*, *Haiku Scotland*, *Harvests*, *The Heron's Nest*, *A Hundred Gourds*, *Kokako*, *Lynx*, *Modern English Tanka*, *moonset*, *Page Seventeen*, *paper wasp* (including the Jack Stamm Haiku Award), *Pre-Scribe*, *Presence*, *Prune Juice*, *red lights*, *Ribbons*, *Shamrock*, *Simply Haiku*, *Stylus Poetry Journal*, *Tasmanian Times*, *Wisteria* and *Yellow Moon*.

Other poems in this book were originally published in these anthologies: *Catzilla!*, *Food for Thought*, *Grevillea and Wonga Vine* and *The Melody Lingers On*.

A bird-loving man: haiku and tanka
ISBN 978 1 74027 800 3

First published 2013
Reprinted 2015

GINNINDERRA PRESS
PO Box 3461 Port Adelaide SA 5015
www.ginninderrapress.com.au

Contents

Foreword **7**

Haibun **9**
Heartcourt Spring 11

Haiku **13**

Sequences **33**
Cormorant surfacing 35
In driftwood 36
Red desert dust 38
Lease paddock gate 40
Between headlands 42
Songs from southern seas 44
No net for sparks 46
Intensive care 48
Canada dreaming 50

Tanka **53**

Tanka Prose **81**
On the fourth day 83

my late sister
on a sponsor's plaque
at the aquarium
so delicate a surprise
that leafy sea dragon

In memory of Janet and Hazel

Foreword

Writing haiku and tanka has long been a passion central to my life, in pursuit of clear, resonant images of the natural world and human nature.

Most of this work was published in journals or anthologies across Australia, Austria, Canada, England, Ireland, Scotland, Japan, New Zealand and the United States: I am grateful to all editors involved, including the late Janice M. Bostok, as well as Amelia Fielden, Lorin Ford, M. Kei, Lyn Reeves, Cynthia Rowe and Katherine Samuelowicz, but especially Beverley George and Patricia Prime. Other pieces first appeared in the book *Rural Dwellings – Gippsland and Beyond* (2008): thanks once again to the painter Otto Boron.

It has been a joy to collaborate with a second visual artist, Helen Timbury. My gratitude also goes to Jo McInerney and Anne Outhred for their great help in preparing this selection. Members of Baw Baw Writers' Network – including Tanya Dawes, Lisa Demos, Bill Frew, Jeannie Haughton, Jean Marler and Janet Marsh – make a difference. Other friends to give support include Penelope Asselineau, David Ballantyne, Edwin Batt, Martine Batt, Paul Carter, Iain Colquhoun, Todd Cook, Vaya Dauphin, Guy Dimmick, Kate Driscoll, William Henderson, Sue Heron, Cherie Kilpatrick, Ellen Kochland, Jai Law, Laura McCarthy, James McCaughey, Kathy Meikle, Russell Moyle, Ian Outhred, Peter Roberts, Linton Rousseau, Jill Thompson, Luke Thorneycroft, Sally Walk and Steve Wiegerink. Stephen Matthews at Ginninderra Press also deserves my thanks.

A respect for humanity, nature and language was promoted by my late mother Hazel and older sister Janet: in her children Alistair and Penny, dear Jano lives on. My brother David, younger sister Bronwyn and brother-in-law Mark all affirm my efforts. Without the love and belief of my wife Meg, son Rohan and daughter Sophie, the little birds you see here would never have formed such a flock.

Haibun

Heartcourt Spring

Suggested by a painting of the same title by Otto Boron

Before winter he ringbarked the last gum trees in their home-paddock, just as she fell pregnant again. Now she levers smouldering stumps together with a crowbar. While her eldest pokes a stick at an ant nest near the chimney, her next kicks acid from beneath her diaphragm. Yesterday morning her husband swore he'd be back from town with supplies by nightfall:

an address
that makes her mother smile…
heartcourt spring

Haiku

a fox barks
at the high-plains moon –
creek brisk with thaw

daffodil shoots
through maple leaf mulch ~
first smile

dew drops
on an orb-weaver's web…
spring bulbs in bud

a flame robin
lands on the spade handle –
new snowdrops

city park…
among homing pigeons
a crested native

wattle in bloom
across the mirror lake
dry feathers float

migrant lorikeets
and hometown wattlebirds
squabble for nectar

marmalade cat
sniffing fuchsia flowers…
honeyeater curve

with a spring chill
lambs surround a yard fire ~
mushroom fairy ring

wind-chime tones
from the gazebo
rhythm of rain

streams converging…
beside the riverbank
a python slides

the main canal
flooding reclaimed fields…
no time for tears

vase of jonquils…
clearing from the cellar
that reek of dead rat

headlight glare ~
shielding her cub
a vixen

from oak to elm
owls hoot
full of moon

first sun
on the rocky outcrop
a tiger snake skin

breeding season –
golden-shouldered parrots
in a termite mound

the ewe
nudges her lamb once more ~
ravens cawing

perspiration
where neck meets breast –
string of pearls

forest track ~
before a summer storm
the smell of charcoal

russet sunset…
down a grassy slope
fox cubs wrestling

shadows shift
down an arch of eucalypts ~
rosella sundown

the sheen
on a teal drake's cheek –
bullfrog croaking

New Year's Eve
crickets chirping
'Auld Lang Syne'

bushfire haze ~
the full moon rising
citrus

raked hay
sweet on the breeze
her perfume

a goldfinch
teases out thistledown –
soap bubbles floating

white china jug
on a check picnic cloth…
daisy-chain noon

how many summers
by the seaside, how rarely
at the beach?

spinnaker curve
down the beat to windward
a swan

tide ebbing
on the coastal shelf
this pool a lens

an old man
walking an old dog –
Ninety Mile Beach

terns huddled
on the sandbar…
lone surfer

dusk on the cape…
the last fisherman
shoulders his rod

cave door in the cliff –
a fairy martin dips
into darkness

channel lights blink ~
over the headland
a buzz of surf

poacher's lantern –
all around the island
waves whisper

balmy night
across the inlet
shrimp lights bob

high water
in the mangroves
a spoonbill's poise

prawn fleet late…
over the limestone bluff
an osprey hovers

the heron alights
with a wide slow loop
fly-casting

flood tide ~
along the jetty
dinghies jostle

cloud shadows
pass over the bald hill –
buzz of flies

shotgun blast –
nothing falls from the sky
except silence

white cockatoos
flexing sulphur crests…
rust-red furrows

south wind
down that ploughed slope
blood-and-bone

donkeys
keeping their ears pricked…
farm for sale

silo spillage ~
native pigeons and galahs
crest to crest

that whistling crack
from an eastern whipbird…
blue gums creaking

old hayshed aslant…
shafts of afternoon sun
through cloud

a rufous fantail
darts at riverside bugs…
peach-pink sunset

dusk by the dam ~
taking one quick peek
the platypus

waterhole twilight –
below cicadas
bullfrogs croak

mosquito whine ~
rattling down the valley
a night-freight

fruit bats
wing through the orchard –
nectarine moonrise

eucalypts breathing ~
a ringtailed possum swings
on a torch beam

trout shapes shift
in a clear tarn ~
melting ice

panning for gemstones
in a high-country stream…
her sapphire eyes

jet aircraft
crossing the Milky Way
a shooting star

barn owl blinking…
a lamp flickers
in the broodmare's stall

corellas creaking…
behind the eastern ridge
a hinge of light

spillway at dawn ~
a kookaburra answers
the cricket

memorial plaque
in her botany garden
the newt pond shimmers

Remembrance Day –
breaking the minute's silence
a raven's caw

eagle circling
the Cathedral Range…
Palm Sunday

easterly breeze…
the Tibetan prayer flags
flutter their colours

harmonica ghost –
African hands cup a match
to blow smoky blues

flecks of mud
across my son's freckles…
tadpole jar

the pond brimful
with last spring's ducklings ~
first school day

boy up north…
his father borrows
an atlas

the lilting trill
from a cockatiel…
daughter calling

his son's old room –
from the ceiling little stars
still twinkle-twinkle

chimney smoke
blending with morning mist…
a twin in each arm

that same sweet phrase ~
rustling through leaf mulch
a song thrush

falling acorn –
the blue jay harries
a squirrel

whooping crane
finds its feet in the gulf ~
winter haven

cold front looming –
a red hen scratches
between graves

peak of snow
the hoary marmot whistles
for a crowd

cooling pond mist…
behind the power station
a copper moon

shortest day ~
an eastern yellow robin
lights up the cape

winter solstice –
no rest since you slept
that longest sleep

sails tilt eastward ~
this thirtieth parallel
clear to Chile

trade winds
off the continental shelf
a sperm whale spouts

yacht's mast
slanting with the breeze
an albatross

bay regatta –
fluttering shearwaters
take on the lead boat

across the lagoon
oystercatchers squabble…
still no reply

through reeds
a purple swamphen ~
the creak of oars

the pumice crater
above caldera lakes
alpine daisies

earth tremor ~
black-faced sheep sniff
the stone-wall

volcanic lip –
beneath a waning sun
the crow

Labour Day break ~
across molten bitumen
a black snake slides

truck overtaking –
the curve of its hubcap
reflects this whole car

beyond the plain
one destination…
the sky

black crow
within a kangaroo carcase ~
petrol gauge low

stockmen's hut
by the high-plains track
a wild horse snorts

a palomino
colt tosses his tail…
wisp of cloud

twilight –
already today
is electric

le crépuscule –
déjà aujourd'hui
est électrique

an east wind blowing clouds blue

the crest of this hill the sea

acorns beneath a memorial for the fallen

library time –
a young boy reads
the fish tank

school camp ~
into their own reflections
canoes capsize

border town bus stop ~
a teenage couple waits
for tomorrow

he fills her glass
right up to its brim –
surface tension

dessert menu ~
a new couple risking
sticky date pudding

below the belt …
her snakeskin stiletto
bites his shin

awaiting her call…
in the alley below
a tomcat yowls

church recital ~
on the soprano's breast
a scarlet shimmer

new moustache –
his other
mid-life crisis

middle-age now ~
my hairdresser asks
eyebrows too, sir?

a shadow
of his former self …
quarter-moon

holiday ends
stitching a button
back on this shirt

mother's hoardings…
a letter from a stranger
signed by me

loose button…
Grandma tells her oldest tale
as if new

electrical store ~
the golfer misses his putt
on fifteen screens

Italy at last –
her tourist snap straightens
that leaning tower

photographing
each other photographing
each other

waking rough –
he wins this latest debate
with himself

old hippy searches
genealogy sites…
still finding himself

letter-box ~
today's only mail
an acorn

salt-pan moon…
as her cab draws away
no looking back

Sequences

Cormorant surfacing

A tanka sequence from Cape Conran and the village of Marlo, at the mouth of the Snowy River, on the East Gippsland coast of Victoria

For my daughter Sophie

from the cape
we watch for humpbacks
breaching
bound south for summer ice ~
ears straining for whale song

yacht under sail
beyond the river-mouth
with its slow beat
over the sandbar
a heron plays pilot

a fourth call
from your brand-new love…
our last stay
by the sea together
as father and daughter

tossed by surf
into tideline kelp
this lightest
pebble of pumice…
laughter alongside loss

past the pier
a cormorant surfacing
well away
from where it dived –
your message safely home

In driftwood

A haiku/tanka interchange from Byron Bay and the NSW Northern Rivers

For Meg

brahminy kite
above the breakwater…
copper in your smile

sisters drowning
turned to stone as warning ~
a sign names
tribes that occupied this coast
their kin scratching out that *d*

breaching whales
guide calves south in spring –
daughter in Munich

rainbow
lorikeets in red
bottlebrush…
dreads braided with beads
before yoga

flames leap
from fields of sugar on dark…
brush of hand on skin

dog yelping
at a wave to toss
back his ball ~
young master intent
on castle and moat

glimpse of dolphin
beyond the river mouth…
friends a youth ago

osprey
nest-platform high
by the river…
her house crowded by cane
a girl fishes broad water

busker
picks out a lean old boogie…
temporary tattoo

pelicans
over Broken Head ~
mobile reefs
in spray as humpbacks
slap their tail-flukes

surfer
cuts the crest of a swell…
morning's first latte

on Brunswick beach
she carved me a big sky
in driftwood –
three decades later
I fossick through jetsam

east to the Andes ~
Cape Byron lighthouse
blinks at the dusk

Red desert dust

A tanka/haiku road trip interchange through Menindee to Broken Hill and back

With thanks to David B

eroding this bend
the river in full flow…
still upright
these trees hold on for dear life
half their roots treading water

pastoral lease ~
bisecting the salt pan
a fence-line

the last flood
marked on each tree trunk
in silt…
a picnic-ground red gum
with its coolamon scar

wildlife sighting –
emus cross the saltbush plain
to check us out

a spot to pan
through alluvial sand
for gemstones
by the Darling's banks
a pair of diamond doves

desert lakes brimful…
two shingleback lizards fight
mouth to mouth

Daydream Silver Mine ~
waist high with a canvas roof
this rough stone hut
once home to eight-year-olds
sorting ore below ground

street tyres
sliding through red desert dust
a western brown snake

by the junction
of those two biggest rivers
a paddle-steamer
under reconstruction –
nearby a canoe tree

kangaroo country…
in our headlights dead in front
tonight's fifth owl

back home down south
no Sturt's desert peas
just roses
this red centre sand
still stuck to my boots

Lease paddock gate

A Gippsland haiku sequence prompted by the painting *Cattle Farm – Victoria Hills* by Otto Boron

peregrine glance…
through the lease paddock gate
an angus herd spreads

cold front
over the back ridge ~
new tractor

crow caw –
a black cow grazes
near afterbirth

irrigator arc
over furrows bleeding…
tiger snake hiss

bread oven-fresh
for a harvest lunch ~
sweet hay breeze

miscarriage…
a dead sapling's ghost
afloat on the dam

cicada buzz
from the poplar break…
farm loan due

mirage shimmer
on the sale yards road…
beef prices down

broken windmill…
a trickle of sweat
between breasts

mosaic in clay
across the dam floor…
shotgun finger

her smile
thin on return ~
new moon

Between headlands

A haiku string from New Zealand's North and South and Stewart Islands

a sloping field
below the abattoir
sunflowers at dawn

fern glade…
a fantail pivots
around its fan

clouds parting
above the crater lake
a volcano

snowy peaks ~
hung from roadside barbed wire
the bodies of stoats

whale-boat
its ribs bare to the wind
a dead seal

muttonbirds
skimming
the sea
shifts

dolphins leap
between headlands
the ocean

her smile all week
at talk of his visit –
through this strait a gale

ferry terminal ~
across the pier's empty deck
a thump of spray

rufous falcon
winding down through that gorge
this river in jade

shingle beach…
trying out its third couple
a dog lost at dusk

Songs from southern seas

A tanka sequence from the South and Stewart Islands, New Zealand

For Meg

off the pole
a southerly buster
up the spine
of this isthmus
a lighthouse surprise

night surf humming
below the balcony…
that pitch and roll
from this morning's ferry
still makes our mattress sway

seal pups
by the mouth of the cave
in a pool
splashing each other
a pair of blonde girls

blue cod boat
nearing the safety of port ~
an albatross
signals its homeward course
with semaphore wingspans

by the wharf
two boys leaning forward
to catch balls
behind their backs…
the island's fleet unloads

cemetery
overlooking estuary
and ocean –
we pause beside graves
marked *lost at sea*

No net for sparks

A Gippsland tanka sequence arising from the painting *Dwindling Dwellings* by Otto Boron

waking up
stiff with steam
at dawn ~
on the black spur
a bellowing bull

bloody earth
wounded by harrow
and disc ~
when you cut my skin
it makes me heal

north winds
scorching through boundary
fences –
no net for sparks
in barbed wire

same gamble
in facing a bushfire
as loving ~
to stay and fight
or leave and live?

farmers
in fire trucks chase a shift
in breeze ~
down the front gully
roast beef on the hoof

ploughed field
a firebreak that saved
the old shack…
this land renewed
by flame once again

round bales
across a sloping field
scattered…
faces of you
appearing at random

Intensive care

A tanka sequence from San Francisco, California

In loving memory of my sister Janet

raccoon
on the garage roof below ~
at three
in the morning
the hospital rings once more

I'm going to leave
o-old Texas now…
our goodbye song
from a distance called childhood
sung in intensive care

flat line –
my brother
in law
tenderly brushes
my sister's hair

white egret
by the bay bridge
freeway…
no more beeping now
from that bedside monitor

big sister
born in nineteen fifty-four
gone at fifty-four ~
don't anyone dare ask me
what equals six times nine

planning
her mother's funeral
my niece hums
'The Battle Hymn
of the Republic'

my nephew
farewells his gardener mother
with a poem
from her first home ~
red roses turning to white

plane through cloud
over the Golden Gate
bridge
a hummingbird
shares this air

our last day here –
my younger sister
re-potting cacti
while I plant daffodils
in a time we're calling fall

Canada dreaming

A haiku/tanka interchange: Vancouver, British Columbia – Banff, Alberta

In tribute to my sister Janet (1954–2008)

wild ducks migrating –
dreams shared in a foreign land
named childhood

city skyline
across the bay
bursting
from the water's edge
a pair of sandpipers

totem-pole shadow…
beneath the woodpecker's beak
sawdust drifting

first-nation shore –
a shard of beer-bottle glass
tumbled
smooth and sharp
as an arrowhead

spring water purling ~
a bull elk in velvet
rubs antlers

in the shallows
a great blue heron
alert
ready to snap
with this lens

from a pine
the red-tailed hawk alights…
gondola drop

twin members
of a first tribe gazing
in sepia
beyond the far shore
Canada geese head south

on gnarled trunks
ferns sprout from moss –
beaver dam

a raft of logs
forming up on the river
as lumberjacks skip…
too late to see Canada
together now sister

maple leaves falling ~
this rocky mountain stream
red with salmon

Tanka

a bird-loving man
in a house fond of felines…
our daughter's cat
rattling the screen door
drops a parrot at my feet

old she-cat
back home at last
such outrage
in her miaowing
this famine all my fault

within a fortnight
both our mothers gone…
grimalkin
gives me a cuff without claws
our last feisty old girl

her pair
of Siamese cats
each head to tail
within one basket ~
yin-and-yang sign

hackles up
hissing whiskers to snout
our son's cat Toby
shows this upstart pup who's boss…
a new soft-toy from Gran

black
cockatoos fly low
overhead
a toddler points
waving bye-bye

canteen duty
again this weekend –
serving hotdogs
she misses her son
score his first-ever goal

with that tilt
of her smiling eyes
long loved
from a baby snap
she plans her overseas trip

message
from my daughter
on the train
stranger opposite
reading your book

river mist ~
from his research lab
our son calls
while waiting on
an evaporation

cheapest rail fare
from Paris to Madrid
overnight
waking drowsy from ether
backpack gutted by blades

magpies at dawn…
from across the dateline
our son
answers my call
direct from yesterday

in late summer
high in a dead tree
four eagles…
our son and daughter
both gone for good

a bike ride north
towards the divide
at sunset
the west wind blows
my shadow longer

moonrise
stretching shadows
further
up the slope
a stag in antler

wild horses
splashing through a ford
at full gallop –
above the razorback
smoke in a corkscrew

in horsehair
on the fire track
a bird's nest ~
this north wind scorching
the back of my throat

burnt-out car
after the bushfire –
by her side
on the passenger seat
a set of bone china

this dispute
over territory
black and white
a nesting mudlark
chasing a magpie

weighbridge
beside the highway ~
from the ditch
a road-kill owl
keeps its eye right on me

jabiru's beak
deep in mangrove mud
probing…
almost scot-free till that
last awkward question

cattle egrets
pecking at grasshoppers
under hooves…
from neighbouring driveways
we both sweep camellias

each spring
the dread of pruning
this hedge…
a bird's nest
pink with chicks

magpies warbling
between currawongs
whistling –
wake-up calls
in counterpoint

the rump
of a chestnut harrier
so white
these coastal peaks
under snow all summer

inshore
a war canoe carved red
at anchor
out between islands
a white ocean liner

three-metre swell
in a treacherous strait…
even labels
for the island's vintage
glued to bottles at a tilt

tide rising
on the sandstone shelf
at dusk
we follow in the footsteps
of dinosaurs

upstairs
at her window
a girl
in silhouette –
on the river the moon

firetail
finches rouge-red in rump
brow and beak ~
seeding grassland astir
with this hint of her lips

still here
beside the dam
at sunset
this copper shelduck hen…
on the bus that girl once more

full moon back
after an eclipse
by cloud…
such beauty now
years after parting

chestnut-breasted
the spinebill siphons
nectar…
a toast for the bride
her tan salon-bronze

at the soak
a flock of desert parrots
on dusk
she makes her way home
surprised by his smile

stiff with sheen
creaking as we stretch
straight off the shelf
a brand new pair of shoes
yet to break each other in

bay window
in the nursery –
watching
blackbirds with young
as she breast-feeds

wedge-tails
spiral overhead
in tandem
on an updraft of our own
we brush outstretched wings

wine-red
our Japanese maple
old
as this golden ring ~
silver anniversary

bird's nest
high in a bare poplar…
death notice
for an old love
last seen by a grave

with his first crow
our young cockerel
tentative
heralds a birthday dawn
far from my first

old soul songs
fine as ever in your car ~
I try
whistling in harmony
free as a younger love

concert
of a lifetime –
he opens up
with my favourite tune
the following night

a yearning blues
pitched in a minor key
at the old hall
that shook and rocked and rolled
when I first kissed a girl

Latin sound
in its rhythm
sinuous
she dances alone
in a room full of partners

Bach recital ~
from its great pipe organ
the chapel
throbs with pillars of sound
between columns of stone

a brass band
in the rotunda
thumping –
every salvation song
much the same

harmonica
blowing at Saltwater River…
blue wind
through a roofless row
of cellars that held felons

in the park
a troupe of jugglers
practising –
everything still
up in the air

the gleam of rings
as boys shape to spar
by streetlight ~
beneath a wharf beacon
the glint of barramundi

your flag
with a shift of wind
gives a clap…
between black sky and red earth
a gold disc dawning

young carver
of tribal totems
pressing his cheek
against the grain
of his forefathers

Lake Pedder lost
from Van Diemen's Land –
Huon pines
alive before Christ
flooded for this hydro scheme

trees torn
from the cliff-top
by storms ~
down on the tide line
a single oar

a canyon gouged
towards city and sea ~
this creek
glinting through redwoods
dives beneath concrete

eyes stinging
from grit at gale-force…
sandpipers
between clumps of kelp
can still play hide-and-seek

outdoor café
on the water's edge –
surrounded
by river wardens
pigeon sparrow and gull

low tide
on the mangrove flats –
from dark holes
blue mud-crabs sneaking
a sideways glance

neon
from the night-ferry
shimmering
across the strait ~
aurora australis

hermit crab…
asleep at noon
on the street
he risks one foot bare
his right shoe a pillow

Jack Kerouac Lane
behind City Lights Books ~
a brother hauls
his home in plastic
pressed by three squad cars

age rings in cedar…
with a second-hand volume
of Beat poems
an air-ticket bookmark
years late for boarding

self-sown
tomatoes sprouting…
from the dresser
hangs last year's calendar
birthdays circled in red

flowing again
after seven years' drought…
a rowing club
walks the river's water-head
back down its dry straight

a broad reach
of rocky mountain stream
pink with sockeye –
on the wing all at once
I count fifteen osprey

fairy-wren
azure in cheek and brow
cobalt in bib
its brown wings bringing
the sky down to earth

parrots
crimson green and blue
surging
dipping and weaving
my heart's shades and paths

with a glint
the rainbow bee-eater swoops…
dry winds
around stalks of spinifex
tracing circles in sand

shimmering
on the desert track
a mirage
her smile radiant
for the man behind me

ominous
air this morning…
a storm
threatening
until you wink

between waves
silver gulls flying low
with a squall
in the hallway next day
we each avert eyes

shellfish trails swirl
across a film of sand
over stone
in a tidal pool…
reading coded sorrows

spotted trout
in a clear mountain stream
head-on
against the current
I likewise hold my line

jolted
from daydream
your eyes
white with alarm…
the pheasant takes flight

winter moon
one night shy of full…
that blink
of hesitation
before her reassurance

an east wind
blows this surf beach bare
of fish ~
no bites when I cast
for the gleam of your teeth

a trawler
beyond the harbour
turning
slowly by degrees
away from her door

this straight road
beyond the next ridge
out of line
first her question
then his reply

frosty ride ~
beneath a roadside blackwood
on this slope
I place a boobook owl
made warm by morning sun

overhead
through mountain grey gums
the shreal
of gang gang cockatoos ~
a rusty hinge creaking

a flutter of wings
on the fringe of vision ~
turning quickly
towards its shadow
I miss the bird behind me

aviary
without wire…
you fly
towards jungle
a bird of paradise

I return
to the site of my first home
now bare
to pitch a tent
across youth and loss

a stranger
appearing in this room
surely locked…
don't be scared   waking boy
by the man you'll become

that whiff of brine
off the river-mouth…
from youth
my best of friends
now a stranger

glass marble
with a helix in blue ~
harvesting
from my vegetable plot
another man's childhood

with blackbirds
perched on each shoulder
the old scarecrow
guards the berry patch
his heart in the job no more

from a dream
where you're driving me
to be hanged
I wake still singing
'Green green grass of home'

the float
sucked below the surface
bobs back up
without a catch...
awake again too soon

pink clouds
to the east
at dawn ~
that shepherd's warning
to turn my day around

you celebrate
your fiftieth birthday
with jet-lag ~
one way to avoid
our shortest day of the year

tinnitus
ringing shrill in my ears ~
at last
I concede it's time
to listen to myself

well-weighted
your last bowl draws close
to the jack…
alive in you, my uncle,
the father I scarcely knew

trees on their sides
after storms through the forest
some roots still holding ~
still hoping dear daddy
you'll come back some day

within a week
of his father's funeral
she leaves…
first Hiroshima
and then Nagasaki

mist
on the cooling pond ~
I climb
to Grandpa's grave
not finding Father's headstone

a swallow
skims its own reflection
beneath the bridge…
recalling the night
when I too might have leapt

old marking gauge
still scribing lines in timber
parallel
to a leading edge ~
boyhood gift from Father

up the hill
our neighbour's axe
falls –
a second of silence
while sound chases light

in a field
flanked by plum trees
a chimney
its wood-fire stove
burning with rust

mist
on southern foothills
snow
north on the ranges
laughter at your hearth

a jersey herd
golden on the river flats
at sunset
my uncle smiles
harvesting his last hay

homestead
slaughterhouse
sagging
under the weight
of rust and blood

big rigs
down the highway
all night
cows bellow
for lost calves

on harvest
potato bags stand full
by red furrows…
in fields far to the west
long rows of white crosses

cliff swallows
back to nest on mission walls –
gipsy potters
with no taste for wine
making their bottles home

welcome
reward in a short story
contest ~
with the prize-money
she buys a front-door mat

footprints
on an empty beach
approaching
homeward bound
I run into myself

Squeaky Beach ~
near his mother's ashes
my nephew snaps
his shadow stretching
across noisy sand

gliding low
over highway one
an eagle…
sister's first birthday
since her passing

Judith you lived
sixty winters ago
for thirteen days –
grief for possibility
my youngest eldest sister

silverware
against porcelain
softens
butter chilled to stiffness ~
Gran's wink across time

frail hands
that taught me how to wield
knife and fork
let me cut your meat
for Mother's Day

a call
from Mum in the depths
in her eighties…
happy Father's Day, son
one week too soon

mother lapsing
into dementia…
with her cook's cup
made of sea-green glass
I dole out porridge oats

a squirrel
storing acorns
Mum conceals
half-eaten shortbreads
inside her glasses' case

on its edge
a silver coin spinning…
Gran mistakes
her youngest son
for her baby brother

the recessional
to end our mother's service –
my sister
ducks back to collect
her own sprig of rosemary

the first weekend
since Mum's funeral –
these hills
surrounding our hometown
all echo in silence

daffodils in bud
after scarcely a bloom
in years…
this anniversary
of Mother's passing

Tanka Prose

On the fourth day

with the breeze
one sleeve from a blouse
rising
above the clothesline…
mother calls me brother

Late on the first day of her dying, our mother's condition improves, such that she is about to be returned to the dementia unit where she has lived for the last two years. As an ambulance officer wheels a gurney through the bustle of the hospital's emergency department, Mother notes that this fellow has found an answer to the shortage of beds here – he's brought his own…

With my sister and me each at work once more, and with our mother safe in her own room, the second day becomes a rest break from high blood pressure.

Needing an ambulance again on the third morning, Mother's eyes widen with a stab. For a moment or two she seems to leave us. Emergency staff converge from all directions, bringing her back with a jolt. The unit manager tells us that our dear old one is dying. My sister and I agree not to resuscitate.

Across the remaining day and night, into the following afternoon, our mother will never wake again. Never speak another word. Never smile once more.

Placed in a withdrawal room – against the beep and flicker of monitors – she holds on, as we each hold her hands. No change.

Moved to a ward, Mother is visited by dear friends, our closest cousin, both my children deep in the middle of the night. At least one of us remains by her side at all times. At three a.m., I read her a poem written in tribute to her long before – at its final line, she raises one last appraising eyebrow. While my sister massages her palm from a bedside chair, I fall asleep on a foam mattress on the floor. Still no change.

Before dawn on the fourth day, a palliative care nurse warns us that loving families need to let the dying die. Later, others affirm that we will show our love best by letting her go…

After our first break together for coffee, my sister and I return, only to hear a loud rasp in Mother's breath. A change at last – we feel guilty in feeling relieved. Sensing that we should not stop what we have allowed to begin, once more we leave her be.

So that she might be no longer…

When we return soon afterwards, a curtain has been drawn across her doorway. We find Mother still and silent: her complexion grey; her mouth wide open; her face without covering. Rushing out for help, I urge the resident to come quickly, as our mother might well have died.

I know, the young doctor replies – I've just signed her death certificate:

the old skiff
in need of dry dock
starts sinking
despite baling…
a nurse's hands in ours

www.ingramcontent.com/pod-product-compliance
Lightning Source LLC
Chambersburg PA
CBHW062145100526
44589CB00014B/1686
9781740278003